# Kitchen Conversions

# Kitchen Conversions

## Carmen Wilde

# Contents

# Introduction

Cooking and baking can often feel overwhelming, especially when it comes to accurately measuring ingredients. In this guide, we'll explore the different ways to measure ingredients and the situations that call for certain methods. You'll learn about volume measurements, conversions, and the differences between various world standards. We aim to demystify the methods available for home cooks to measure more accurately, even without a kitchen scale. Additionally, you'll find helpful charts for quick reference in your home cooking, making this guide an essential tool for every kitchen.

## The Importance of Accurate Measurements

One of the most challenging aspects of cooking and baking is the simple act of measuring out ingredients. For some, it can feel downright frustrating, if not intimidating. However, virtually every professional chef and home cook alike agrees that one crucial key to measuring out ingredients accurately—no matter your experience or comfort level in the kitchen—is to weigh your ingredients with a digital kitchen scale. We believe there are many great reasons to have a kitchen scale at home: it ensures precision, reduces waste, and helps achieve consistent results.

## The Convenience of Measuring Spoons and Cups

That said, we also appreciate the convenience of using measuring spoons and cups, especially when you want to throw together a quick batch of pancakes or follow a recipe that doesn't require exact measurements. This guide will be helpful for those who prefer the ease of measuring spoons and cups, as well as for those interested in using both size and weight measurements together for increased accuracy.

**Purpose of the Guide**

This guide is specifically created for individuals who are new to cooking or baking and are unsure about the precise measurements and quantities they should use when preparing ingredients.

**Focus on Weight Measurements**

For clarity, this guide will focus on weight measurements for those living in the UK, Ireland, and countries using the metric system. It will also feature corresponding metric-to-imperial conversions and ingredient-based conversions. This allows those who prefer to understand an ingredient's necessary weight based on how many there are in a pound or the equivalence of two cups of flour in grams to do so seamlessly.

**Detailed Conversion Charts and Guides**

Contained within this guide is a comprehensive list of dry goods—including flour, sugar, various types of sugar, and butter or spreads—and their corresponding weights in grams and ounces. You'll also find a simple, user-friendly conversion chart, information on using liquid measuring jugs for both volume and weight, and conversions to cups and millilitres.

**A Resource for All Cooks**

This guide aims to help new cooks who may have been tasked with preparing meals for the household or baking during the Covid-19 lockdown and need to follow recipes that call for weight measurements in grams or millilitres. By breaking down the confusion around weight measurements, we aim to ensure that all valid questions are answered. This guide is designed as a hub of information for anyone uncertain about cooking measurements, enabling them to cook or bake independently using recipes featuring unfamiliar units.

# 1

## *Chapter 2: Basic Cooking Measurements*

Cooking measurements are essential to the success of any recipe. Often, if a recipe is not followed exactly, an entire dish could be ruined. Any baker who's accidentally used tablespoons of salt instead of sugar can attest to this. There are two primary types of measurements used in the kitchen: **volume measurements** and **weight measurements**. Volume measurements are used for liquids, segregated solids, and dry ingredients that can be leveled, like flour. Examples of volume measurements include pints, quarts, gallons, and cups. Weight measurements, expressed in ounces, pounds, and grams, convert various ingredients into a common base unit.

**Units of Weight and Volume**

In the list of units for weight and volume, measurements are grouped into standard, multiple, and fractions of the personal cup. A standard unit of measure is the most used quantity and the building block for other measurements in the same category. A multiple of the measure is the increasing standard unit amount. A smaller measure is a fraction of the standard unit. These fractions can still be good round numbers. Understanding the technique of cooking measurements shows you how much of an ingredient is needed to be successful. We'll backstack the basic measurements and definitions onto the next section, where we will discuss conversion factors and specialized conversions to use in the kitchen.

**Volume Measurements**

When you measure liquids or other bulk foods, you are typically working with units of volume. In everyday speech, we call these units teaspoons, quarts, etc. In the United States, we sometimes put ounces in this list, though in fact, the term is actually not a volume term but a weight term (see below). Commercial recipes and large-scale kitchen manufacturing typically use the metric system, and the basic metric unit of volume is the milliliter (mL).

- **Teaspoon (tsp):** A teaspoon is 1/3 of a tablespoon or 1/6 of a fluid (liquid) ounce. In the US, a teaspoon holds about 4 ml, whereas in the United Kingdom and some Commonwealth countries such as Australia and India, a teaspoon holds exactly 5 ml.
- **Tablespoon (tbsp):** A tablespoon is 3 teaspoons, 1/2 of a fluid ounce, or 1/16 of a cup. In the US, a tablespoon is approximately equal to 1/2 fluid ounce or three teaspoons, whereas in the United Kingdom and some other countries, the tablespoon is about 20% smaller.
- **Fluid Ounce (fl oz):** One US fluid ounce is 1/8 of a cup, 2 tablespoons, 6 teaspoons, or 1/16 of a US pint or 1/32 of a US quart. One Imperial (British) fluid ounce is 1.20 of a US fluid ounce or 1/20 of a British pint.
- **Cup (c):** A cup is 8 fluid ounces, 16 tablespoons, or 48 teaspoons. This is commonly used in US recipes.
- **Pint (pt):** A liquid pint is 2 cups, 4 gills, 8 fluid ounces, or 1/2 of a quart. In the US, a pint is equal to 1/8 of a gallon or 16 fluid ounces.

- **Quart (qt):** A liquid quart is 2 pints, 4 cups, 32 fluid ounces, or 1/4 of a gallon. In the US, a quart is equal to 1/32 of a bushel, 1/4 of a peck, or 1/16 of a dry gallon.
- **Gallon (gal):** A liquid gallon is 4 quarts, 8 pints, 16 cups, 128 fluid ounces, or 3.785 liters. In the US (but not in the UK), a gallon is divided into fourths and called a "quart", which contains 2 pints each.

### Weight Measurements

In the U.S., we have a tradition (some might call it a bad habit) of measuring nearly all our ingredients in volume. This is a holdover from our early days as a nation when most people didn't have accurate scales, but they did have graduated containers that could be used to measure the ingredients for a cake. For the home cook, it's certainly handy to scoop a cup of sugar or a spoonful of honey. However, the use of volume measurements for dry ingredients has made baking tricky for many cooks, especially as pre-sifted flours gradually ground to a halt on supermarket shelves across the U.S. This dichotomy between professional and home cooking in the U.S. leads to real headaches in the kitchen, particularly with vague directions on packaging that call for "1 egg" when nearly all eggs, large or extra-large, vary in grams.

Reassurance should flow from the fact that eggs and liquids are nearly always measured by volume in professional kitchens. Here are some of the most common weight measurements for cooking used today:

- **Ounce (oz):** Weight and volume can often be nearly the same; for example, 1/4 cup = 2 oz (volume) = 4 tablespoons = 12 teaspoons (volume) = 28.35 grams.

- **Pound (lb):** The volume of butter in a pound is 2 cups; salted butter is 1.96 cups (depending on the source). A pound of butter is 454 grams or 4 sticks.

By understanding and utilizing these basic measurements, you can ensure that your cooking and baking efforts are successful, whether you're using volume or weight measurements.

**2**

# *Chapter 3: Conversion Factors*

One key principle to any effective kitchen conversion is the idea of a **conversion factor**. A million teachers, parents of home cooks, and food bloggers alike have defined a conversion factor as "a number used to change one set of units into another set of units." Despite the apparent accuracy suggested by these definitions, they don't explain how to select the conversion factor or why you multiply or divide the numbers in the first place.

**Understanding Conversion Factors**

Volume measurements and weight measurements have a clear relationship, but they are not equivalent. That's precisely where conversion factors come into play. A conversion factor is the number that converts one weight unit into another or one volume unit into another. These factors are derived from the relationships between different units and are based on the multiplication of two relationships that equal one.

For instance, one cup of sugar is 7 ounces and also equals 0.44 pounds. If you want to convert from fluid ounces to pounds, you can use this equation: 1 cup of sugar = 7 oz. ÷ 1 cup of sugar. To cancel out ounces and end with an answer in pounds, you'd multiply your initial conversion factor with consecutive conversion factors, leaving you with pounds.

## Volume to Volume Conversions

Volume to volume conversions can be tricky, especially when recipes are not as exact as baking recipes. Here is a simple way to figure out your conversions:

- **Converting Teaspoons to Tablespoons:** One tablespoon is equal to three teaspoons. When converting teaspoons to tablespoons, divide the number of teaspoons by three. For example, if a recipe calls for 10 teaspoons and you want the equivalent amount in tablespoons, divide 10 by 3, which equals approximately 3.33 tablespoons.
- **Converting Teaspoons to Fluid Ounces:** There are two tablespoons per fluid ounce. To convert teaspoons to fluid ounces, first convert the number of teaspoons to tablespoons, and then to fluid ounces. For example, if a recipe calls for 12 teaspoons, convert to tablespoons by dividing by 3 ($12 \div 3 = 4$ tablespoons), and then divide by 2 ($4 \div 2 = 2$ fluid ounces).

## Common Volume Conversions

- **3 teaspoons (tsp) = 1 tablespoon (tbsp)**
- **16 tablespoons (tbsp) = 1 cup (c)**
- **8 fluid ounces (fl oz) = 1 cup (c)**

## Weight to Weight Conversions

Weight-to-weight conversions are useful when you don't want to use cups and tablespoons for measuring ingredients. For instance, after measuring out a cup of flour, you can use the U.S. Department of Agriculture's numbers to see that one cup of all-purpose flour equals 125 grams. Here are some useful conversions:

- **1 ounce (oz) = 28 grams (g)**
- **1 pound (lb) = 454 grams (g)**
- **3.5 ounces (oz) = 100 grams (g)**
- **4.5 ounces (oz) = 125 grams (g)**
- **1 pound (lb) = 0.45 kilograms (kg)**

## Quick Conversion Example

If a recipe calls for 8 ounces of flour and you want to know the weight in grams:

- **Ingredient amount in one unit:** 8 ounces
- **Given weight in closer unit (USDA says 1 cup flour = 125g):** Multiply 8 ounces by 28 grams/ounce (8 × 28 = 224 grams).

By using these conversion factors, you can ensure accurate measurements, whether you're working with volume or weight.

**3**

# *Chapter 4: Commonly Used Conversions*

**I**ntroduction to Kitchen Conversions
Understanding kitchen conversions is crucial for translating recipes accurately. Whether you're converting measurements from metric to imperial or vice versa, these conversions help ensure precision in your cooking and baking.

**Common Kitchen Conversions**

Here are a few essential kitchen conversions to help translate your recipes:

- **1 cup** = 16 tablespoons (tbsp)
- **1 cup** = 48 teaspoons (tsp)
- **1 tablespoon (tbsp)** = 3 teaspoons (tsp)
- **1 tablespoon (tbsp)** = 15 milliliters (ml)
- **1 teaspoon (tsp)** = 5 milliliters (ml)
- **1 stick of butter** = ½ cup or 8 tablespoons (tbsp)
- **1 pound (lb)** = 16 ounces (oz)
- **1 fluid ounce (fl oz, U.S.)** = 29.6 milliliters (ml)
- **1 pint (pt)** = 16 fluid ounces (fl oz)
- **1 quart (qt)** = 2 pints (pt)

- **1 quart (qt)** = 32 fluid ounces (fl oz)
- **1 gallon (gal)** = 16 cups (c)
- **1 gallon (gal)** = 4 quarts (qt)
- **½ cup** = 4 fluid ounces (fl oz)
- **⅓ cup** = 2 ⅔ tablespoons (tbsp)
- **⅔ cup** = 10 ⅔ tablespoons (tbsp)

## Weight Conversions

- **1 pound (lb)** = 16 ounces (oz)
- **1 ounce (oz)** = 28.3495 grams (g)

## Liquid Measurement Conversions

- **1 quart (U.S.)** ≈ 32 ounces ≈ 1 liter (L)
- **1 cup (c)** = 8 fluid ounces (fl oz)
- **1 pint (pt)** = 16 fluid ounces (fl oz)
- **1 gallon (gal)** = 128 fluid ounces (fl oz)
- **1 milliliter (ml)** = 0.033814 fluid ounces (fl oz)
- **1 liter (L)** = 33.814 fluid ounces (fl oz)

## Temperature Conversions

- **Freezing** = 0° Celsius (C) = 32° Fahrenheit (F)
- **Boiling** = 100° Celsius (C) = 212° Fahrenheit (F)

## Cups to Tablespoons

When it comes to kitchen measurements, we do not always have the appropriate tools at hand. For example, you might come across a recipe requiring a cup of sugar, but you only have a bag of sugar in your cabinet. Without a cup, you might feel lost. The solution? Tablespoons! By converting cups to tablespoons, you can successfully produce your desired kitchen creation.

Cups and tablespoons are two common measurements used in both cooking and baking. One cup is equal to 16 tablespoons, which can easily be used to convert any amount of one ingredient to another. Having the right cup to tablespoon conversion is key to making the final dish great. Both cups and tablespoons come in precise measurements and can only be switched out for each other once the correct conversions have been made.

**Practical Applications**

Converting your measurements is also important when making homemade ice cream in an ice cream maker or when preparing goods in an instant pot. Remember, every chance to increase your organizational capacity in the kitchen will help you avoid common kitchen mishaps that could ruin your recipe.

**Ounces to Grams**

Ounces, a British measurement, are a unit of weight in the U.S. customary and British imperial systems of measurement. There are 16 ounces in one pound, making conversions between ounces and pounds straightforward. Since they break down into smaller units, such as grams, these measurements are necessary for precision in culinary fields, science, health, and medical areas.

While ounces and grams may appear different, 1 ounce is essentially equal to 28.3495 grams.

**Understanding Grams**

A gram (g) is a metric system SI unit of mass. It is the base unit of mass in the metric system, commonly utilized in contemporary scientific and specialized areas. A gram is a hundredth of a kilogram, the fundamental base unit of mass in the metric scheme. The gram itself is divided into a thousand milligrams.

**Practical Applications**

Knowing the equivalent values in grams and ounces is important since various liquids and ingredients have differing masses by volume. Using a standard digital scale with a tare function is recommended during baking and cooking experiments. Familiarizing yourself with these conversions will ensure accuracy and consistency in your culinary creations.

# 4

# *Chapter 5: Specialized Conversions*

**V**olume Conversions
Volume conversions help in translating recipes, especially when dealing with liquid ingredients. Here are some common conversions:

- **1 teaspoon** = 5 milliliters
- **1 tablespoon** = 15 milliliters
- **1/5 cup** = 50 milliliters
- **1/4 cup** = 60 milliliters
- **1/3 cup** = 75 milliliters
- **1/2 cup** = 125 milliliters
- **2/3 cup** = 150 milliliters
- **3/4 cup** = 175 milliliters
- **1 cup** = 250 milliliters
- **1 1/4 cup** = 300 milliliters
- **1 1/3 cup** = 325 milliliters
- **1 1/2 cup** = 375 milliliters
- **2 cups** = 475 milliliters
- **3 1/2 cups** = 900 milliliters

- **4 cups/1 quart** = 1 liter
- **1 pint** = 500 milliliters
- **1 1/4 pint** = 600 milliliters
- **1 1/3 pint** = 650 milliliters
- **2 pints** = 900 milliliters
- **5 pints** = 2.5 liters
- **8 pints/1 gallon** = 4.5 liters

## A Mix of the Two

- **1/8 cup** = 2 tablespoons = 30 milliliters
- **1/4 cup** = 4 tablespoons = 60 milliliters
- **1/3 cup** = 5 tablespoons + 1 teaspoon = 80 milliliters
- **1/2 cup** = 8 tablespoons = 120 milliliters
- **2/3 cup** = 10 tablespoons + 2 teaspoons = 160 milliliters
- **3/4 cup** = 12 tablespoons = 180 milliliters
- **1 cup** = 16 tablespoons = 240 milliliters

## Teaspoons to Milliliters

Understanding the conversion from teaspoons to milliliters is vital for accuracy in cooking, especially with liquid ingredients. The conversion is straightforward:

- **1 U.S. teaspoon** = 4.92892 milliliters (rounded up to 4.93 milliliters for cooking purposes)

For best accuracy, use U.S. standard measuring spoons and liquid measuring cups. In most of the world, the standard teaspoon is considered to be 5 milliliters.

## Practical Application

When following a recipe, particularly for dressings or sauces, precise measurements matter. For instance, if a recipe calls for 1 tablespoon of an emulsion to be drizzled over a salad, using 15 milliliters (one tablespoon) ensures consistency. In practical terms, using 4 teaspoons instead of the precise metric equivalent can lead to irregular flavors.

**Note:** Tablespoon is abbreviated T or tbsp. and Teaspoon is abbreviated t or tsp. As science progresses and test equipment improves, switching between English and metric measurements may become more common.

**Common Teaspoon Conversions**

- **1 U.S. dessertspoon** = 10 milliliters
- **1 U.K. (Imperial) dessertspoon** = 11.2 milliliters

**Pints to Liters**

Pints are commonly used to measure beverages like beer and other liquids. Understanding the conversion between pints and liters is important, especially in culinary and hospitality settings:

- **1 pint** = 0.473176 liter (473.176 milliliters when rounded)

Pints are used for measuring various beverages, and precise conversions are needed for consistency in recipes and serving sizes.

**Practical Application**

In bars and restaurants, beer and wine are often served in pints. In the U.S., a pint of beer is typically 16 ounces, whereas a British pint is 20 ounces. Knowing these conversions helps in ensuring accurate servings and maintaining consistency.

**Quick Reference:**

- **1 U.S. pint** = 473.176 milliliters
- **1 Imperial (British) pint** = 568.261 milliliters

By understanding these specialized conversions, you can ensure precision in your culinary endeavors, whether you're following recipes or serving beverages.

# Chapter 6: Practical Applications

**C**ooking Measurements & Practical Applications

## 1. Making Adjustments

Many cooking implements exist for portion control, ranging from all-in-one nutritional guides to digital bottle-top alcohol tracking systems. While these tools are useful, accurate charts and the masterful use of kitchen math can easily adjust recipes to accommodate large numbers of diners without sophisticated programming. Handy numbers and charts can be just as effective in achieving this. Adjusting recipes to suit different serving sizes, dietary needs, and preferences is often as easy as "pi" (3.14159265) recipes.

## 2. Changing Servings

It's common to find recipes that serve more people than you need or fewer than you want. Adjusting the number of servings isn't limited to increasing or decreasing quantities; it also involves adapting recipes to suit dietary restrictions or preferences. For example:

- **Vegetarian and Vegan Alternatives:** Replace traditional heavy cheese and meat dishes with vegetarian, fat- and cholesterol-free recipes.

- **Allergen-Free Adjustments:** Modify recipes to be dairy-free, gluten-free, or nut-free.
- **Special Events:** When planning large events, calculate enough raw food for 2.2-3.3 servings per person and slightly fewer servings of everyone's favorite dessert to ensure there's enough for all guests.

Personalized recipes can also add a special touch to gatherings by including the names of individuals or groups, making the event even more memorable.

**Recipe Adjustments**

Adjusting recipes while maintaining their intended flavor and texture requires understanding key measurement adjustments. Here are some tips for making effective adjustments:

1. **Liquids:** Adjust by seasonings and adding stock to maintain flavor.
2. **Acids:** Apply the same amount of flavorings as in the original recipe; no adjustment needed.
3. **Leavening Agents:** Use the divide/multiply rule based on the original measurements; no need for separate adjustments.
4. **Fats:** Adjust only if the recipe doesn't require emulsifying fats into other ingredients.
5. **Sugars:** Reduce by half to lower sugar content, but beware of excessive reduction that could disrupt the final product's structure.
6. **Dry Ingredients:** Use techniques like rounded or jam-packed scoops for appropriate conversions.
7. **Flour:** Adjust using the divide/multiply rule based on initial measurements and adjust leavening agents accordingly.

8. **Eggs:** Flexible in home-cooking; a large egg weighs 50 grams (yolk ~18 grams, white ~35 grams). Note the impact on flavor and structure.

## Practical Tips for Adjusting Specific Ingredients

- **Liquids:** Always add seasonings and stock incrementally to preserve the dish's intended flavor.
- **Acids:** Stick to the original quantity to maintain balance in the dish.
- **Leavening Agents:** Follow the divide/multiply rule to ensure proper rise and texture.
- **Fats:** Be cautious with adjustments in recipes requiring emulsification. Mixing in a blender can help with emulsification.
- **Sugars:** Reducing sugar impacts the final product's texture; balance is key.
- **Dry Ingredients:** Use consistent measurement techniques to ensure accuracy.
- **Flour:** Adjust along with leavening agents for consistency in baked goods.
- **Eggs:** Consider the impact of egg adjustments on the dish's final texture and flavor.

Understanding these practical applications and adjustments helps in making informed decisions while cooking and baking, ensuring the best possible outcome for your dishes.

**6**

# *Chapter 7: Conclusion*

**B**ringing It All Together
Whether you are new to the culinary world or just brushing up on basic cooking skills, understanding cooking measurements can make or break your time in the kitchen. As we have learned from this guide, a good cook is thorough in understanding measurements. A knowledgeable cook adds a few more things to their repertoire, such as:

- **Formulating Measurements:** Knowing how measurements are formulated and the importance of measuring ingredients accurately.
- **Converting Measurements:** Mastering how to properly convert measurements will surely enhance your time in the kitchen.

Cooking and baking are meant to be pleasurable and rewarding experiences. Knowing your measurements simply makes it easier to be successful in the kitchen.

**Confidence in the Kitchen**

There you have it: the many measurements, both dry and liquid, that await you on your cooking journey! We hope this guide has given you confidence in your culinary abilities. Converting kitchen measurements can seem intimidating at first, but with practice, it becomes easier.

Meals and baking could not be possible without the wonderful world of measurements. Becoming comfortable using kitchen measurements will make your recipes turn out better, save you time and hassle, and increase your knowledge of the culinary world. Now, head into the kitchen with your newfound knowledge and break out those measuring cups to see what you can whip up!

**Summary of Key Points**

- **Categories of Cooking Measurements:**
    - **Weight:** Measures the mass of an ingredient and is used for dry, dense, or powdered ingredients.
    - **Volume:** Measures the volume of an ingredient and is used for liquids and small, chopped dry ingredients. Each measure is denoted by a spoon or cup of a specific size.
    - **Unit Count:** Counts the individual items or pieces that make up the ingredient, and are also used in reference to ounces, pounds, and gallons.
- **Conversions:**
    - **Definition:** A conversion refers to a specific amount of one ingredient in one form that is equal to a specific amount of an ingredient in another form.
    - **Scaling Factor:** Indicates by how much each of the conversions changes and to what extent two conversions are related.
    - **Finding the Scaling Factor:** For conversions involving weights and volumes, first convert one ingredient

into ounces and the other into ounces, then solve for the scaling factor using the given weights or volumes.
- **Unit Conversions:** To convert between units of the same ingredient in volume and weight, both conversion factors will need to be determined separately.

May you find success and joy in your cooking and baking adventures!